Living in a Biome

Life in a Desert

by Carol K. Lindeen

Consulting Editor: Gail Saunders-Smith, Ph.D.

Consultant: Sandra Mather, Professor Emerita
Department of Geology and Astronomy, West Chester University
West Chester, Pennsylvania

Capstone press

Mankato, Minnesota

Pebble Plus is published by Capstone Press
151 Good Counsel Drive, P.O. Box 669, Mankato, Minnesota 56002
http://www.capstonepress.com

Printed in the United States of America

1 2 3 4 5 6 08 07 06 05 04 03

Library of Congress Cataloging-in-Publication Data
Lindeen, Carol K., 1976–
    Life in a desert / by Carol K. Lindeen.
    p. cm.—(Pebble plus: Living in a biome)
    Summary: Simple text and photographs introduce the desert biome, including
the environment, plants, and animals.
    Includes bibliographical references (p. 23) and index.
    ISBN 0-7368-3399-4 (softcover) ISBN 0-7368-2097-3 (hardcover)
    1. Desert biology—Juvenile literature. [1. Desert biology.] I. Title. II. Series.
QH88 .L55 2004
578.754—dc21   2002155664

Editorial Credits
Martha E. H. Rustad, editor; Kia Adams, designer and illustrator; Juliette Peters, cover production designer; Kelly Garvin, photo researcher;
    Eric Kudalis, product planning editor

Photo Credits
Bruce Coleman Inc./G. Gualco/Union Press, cover
Comstock Klips, 6–7, 14–15
Digital Vision, 1
James P. Rowan, 10–11, 16–17, 18–19
Minden Pictures/Konrad Wothe, 8–9; Michael & Patricia Fogden, 12–13
Robert McCaw, 4–5, 20–21

Note to Parents and Teachers

The Living in a Biome series supports national science standards related to life science. This book describes and
illustrates animal and plant life in a desert. The photographs support early readers in understanding the text. This
book also introduces early readers to subject-specific vocabulary words, which are defined in the Glossary
section. Early readers may need assistance to read some words and to use the Table of Contents, Glossary, Read
More, Internet Sites, and Index/Word List sections of the book.

Word Count: 123
Early-Intervention Level: 12

Table of Contents

What Are Deserts?

Deserts are very dry areas.

They can be hot or cold.

Some deserts are sandy.

Other deserts are rocky.

Deserts are found around

the world.

Deserts

Desert Animals

Camels live in deserts. A camel can live for weeks without drinking water or eating food.

Lizards have dry, scaly skin. Lizards sometimes warm themselves in the sun.

Snakes live in deserts. They
slither across the desert
sands. Snakes hunt for food
at night.

Desert Plants

Shrubs grow in deserts. Shrubs are short, bushy plants.

A cactus has sharp spines.

Cactuses hold water inside

their stems.

Some cactuses and shrubs
have flowers. Desert flowers
bloom when rain falls.

19

Living Together

Desert animals keep cool
in the shade of desert plants.
Desert animals help plants
by spreading seeds.
Deserts are full of life.

Glossary

camel—an animal with a round hump on its back; some camels have one hump, and some have two; camel humps are made of fat.

desert—a very dry area of land; very little rain falls in a desert; deserts can be hot or cold.

scaly—made up of scales; scales are small pieces of hard skin that cover a reptile's body.

shade—an area that is sheltered from sunlight; the air might feel cooler in shady areas.

shrub—a plant or bush with woody stems that branch out near the ground

spine—a sharp, pointed growth on a plant or an animal

stem—the long, main part of a plant from which leaves and flowers grow

Read More

Fowler, Allan. *Cactuses.* Rookie Read-About Science. New York: Children's Press, 2001.

Gray, Susan Heinrichs. *Deserts.* First Reports. Minneapolis: Compass Point Books, 2001.

Trumbauer, Lisa. *What Are Deserts?* Earth Features. Mankato, Minn.: Pebble Books, 2002.

Internet Sites

Do you want to find out more about deserts?
Let FactHound, our fact-finding hound dog, do the research for you.

Here's how:

1) Visit *http://www.facthound.com*

2) Type in the **Book ID** number: **0736820973**

3) Click on **FETCH IT**.

FactHound will fetch Internet sites picked by our editors just for you!

Index/Word List